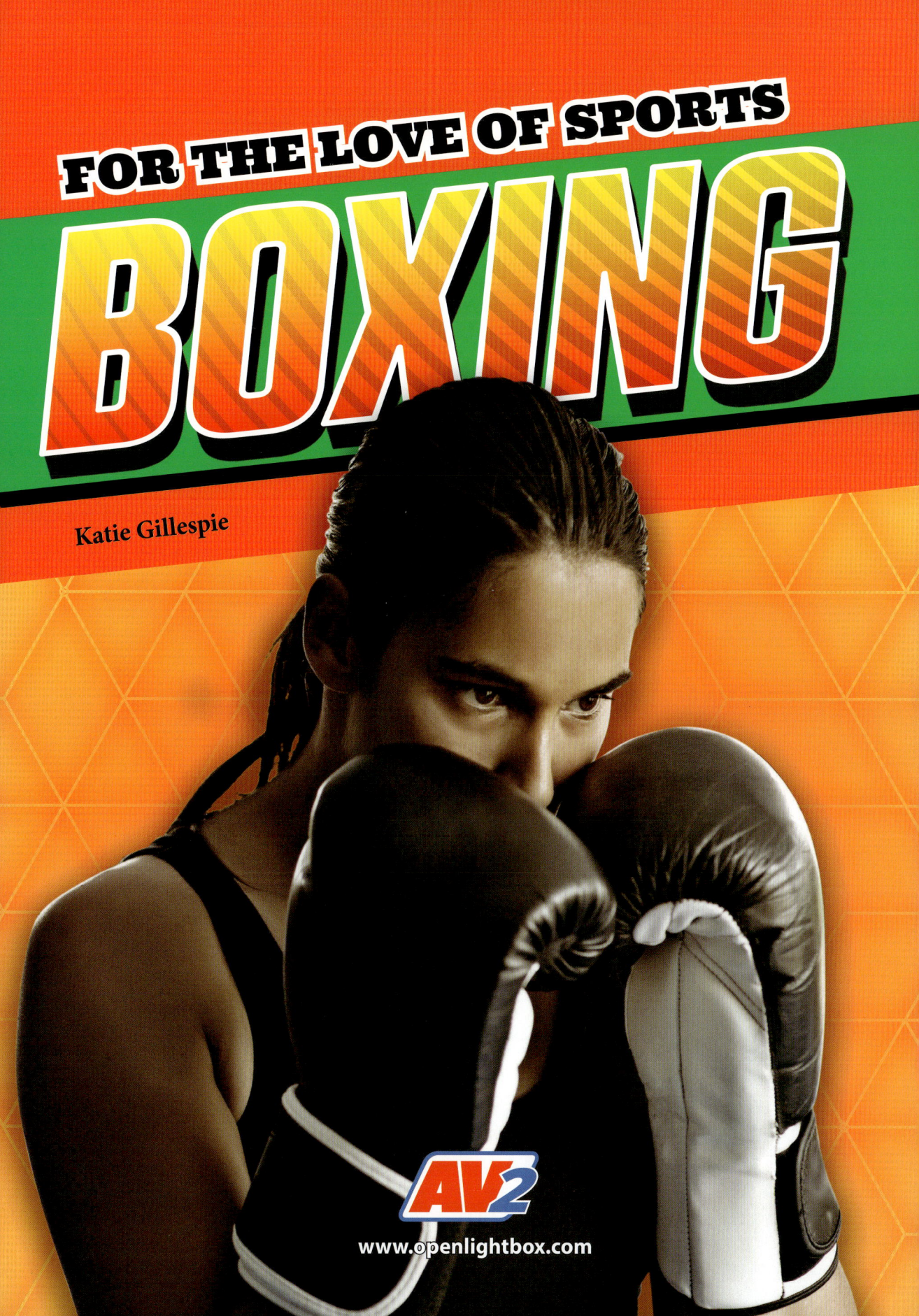

Step 1
Go to www.openlightbox.com

Step 2
Enter this unique code

HVZFER3TK

Step 3
Explore your interactive eBook!

AV2 is optimized for use on any device

Your interactive eBook comes with...

Contents
Browse a live contents page to easily navigate through resources

Audio
Listen to sections of the book read aloud

Videos
Watch informative video clips

Weblinks
Gain additional information for research

Slideshows
View images and captions

Try This!
Complete activities and hands-on experiments

Key Words
Study vocabulary, and complete a matching word activity

Quizzes
Test your knowledge

Share
Share titles within your Learning Management System (LMS) or Library Circulation System

Citation
Create bibliographical references following APA, CMOS, and MLA styles

---

This title is part of our AV2 digital subscription

1-Year Grades K–5 Subscription
ISBN 978-1-7911-3320-7

Access hundreds of AV2 titles with our digital subscription.
Sign up for a FREE trial at www.openlightbox.com/trial

FOR THE LOVE OF SPORTS
BOXING

CONTENTS

- 2   AV2 Book Code
- 4   What Is Boxing?
- 6   Getting Ready to Fight
- 8   The Ring
- 9   Boxing Arenas
- 10 Keeping Score
- 12 Rules of the Ring
- 14 Amateurs and Professionals
- 16 History of Boxing
- 18 Superstars of Boxing
- 20 Staying Healthy
- 22 The Boxing Quiz
- 23 Key Words/Index

What Is Boxing?

Boxing is a combat sport that dates back about 3,000 years. The first formal boxing event was part of the Olympics in ancient Greece. At the time, boxing was known as *pyx*. This Greek word means "with clenched fist."

In boxing, two contestants have a one-on-one physical fight. They try to win the match according to its particular rules. Contestants have to earn points or knock out their opponent.

Boxing matches may have also taken place in ancient Egypt. A relief sculpture featuring boxers was found in the Tomb of Kheruef in Thebes, which was the capital of ancient Egypt.

4   For the Love of Sports

In early boxing matches, **competitors** fought with their bare hands. This "bare-knuckle" boxing was dangerous. However, it was practiced for many years. Padded gloves were not invented until the 18th century.

Over time, more safety rules were developed. Protective equipment was introduced. Eventually, boxing evolved into the kind of **prizefighting** that takes place today. It is popular around the world, both as an **amateur** and **professional** sport for men and women.

Women's boxing has been an official Olympic sport since 2012.

The **fastest boxing match** on record lasted only **four seconds**. It was over in **one punch**.

With a record of **49–0, Rocky Marciano** was the only **heavyweight champion** to retire undefeated.

Claressa Shields is the only American boxer to win consecutive **Olympic** medals, in **2012** and **2016**.

Boxing 5

Getting Ready to Fight

Boxers use a variety of training equipment, including jump ropes and punching bags. Fighters use punching bags to practice their hits. There are many types of punching bags, including heavy bags, speed bags, and double-ended bags. When **sparring**, boxers wear extra safety gear, such as hand wraps and head, body, and groin protectors.

Boxers are required to wear gloves when they fight. Gloves can weigh between 10 and 20 ounces (283 and 567 grams).

Hand wraps are strips of fabric. They are worn under a boxer's gloves. Hand wraps pad the knuckles and support the wrists. Most adults use 180-inch (457-centimeter) wraps.

Mouthguards are important pieces of safety gear that protect the teeth and jaw. Most mouthguards cover only the upper row of teeth.

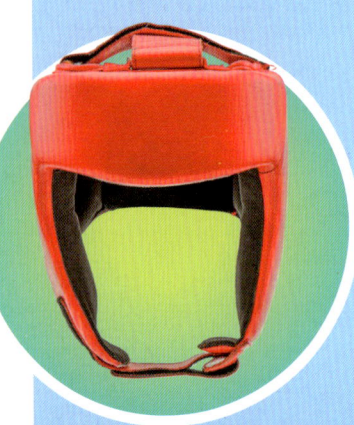

Headgear may be worn to soften blows to the head. It covers the forehead and ears, as well as the back and sides of the head. Headgear is made of padding surrounded by leather.

For the Love of Sports

During a fight, boxers wear trunks. Boxing trunks are like shorts without pockets. Female boxers wear tank tops, too, as do amateur and Olympic male boxers. Shoes with ankle support and a good grip are also important. Protective gear can vary, depending on the level or gender of the participants.

Most men do not wear headgear at any level. Women wear headgear in amateur and Olympic **bouts**, and often in professional boxing matches as well. Before entering the ring, fighters may also wear a robe.

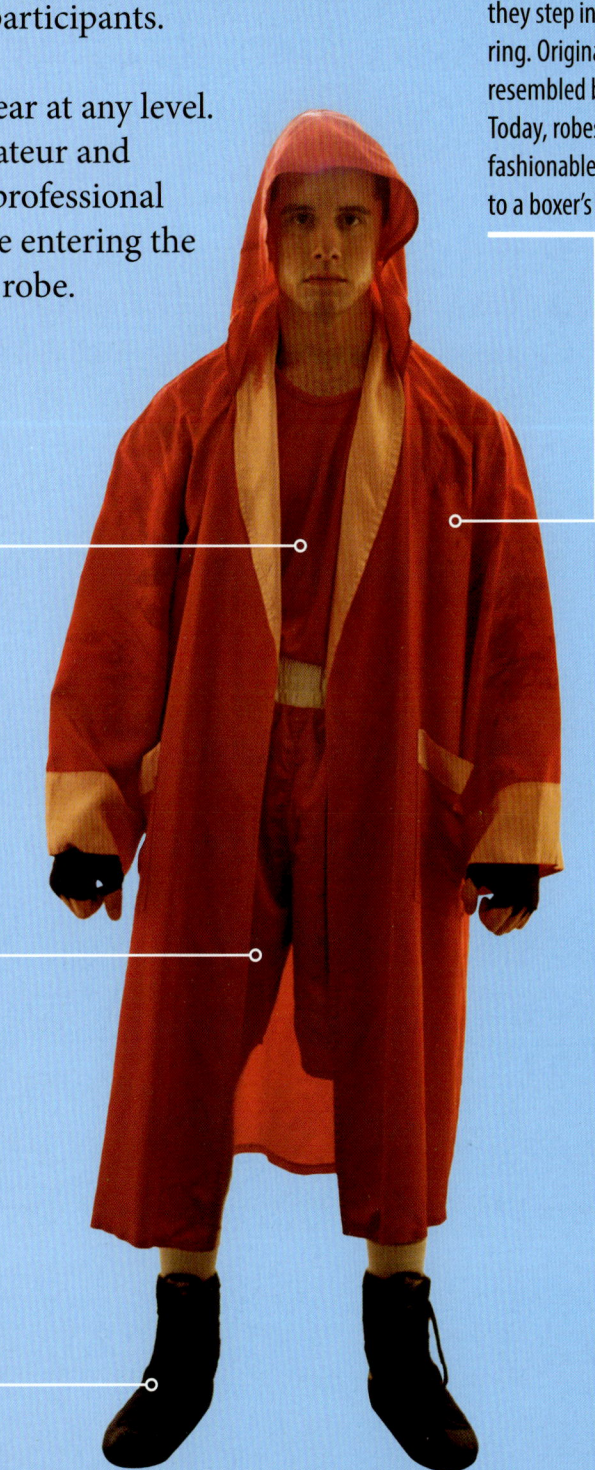

Ring robes keep fighters warm before they step into the ring. Originally, they resembled bath robes. Today, robes are more fashionable and add to a boxer's look.

For boxers who wear them, tank tops protect the body from cuts. Male professionals, who do not wear shirts during bouts, use **petroleum jelly** to reduce friction from punches.

Amateur boxers usually wear blue or red trunks. A professional boxer's trunks may have other colors or embroidery, and often feature the boxer's name on the waistband.

Ring shoes keep fighters from slipping in the ring. They often have rubber soles.

Boxing 7

The Ring

Many years ago, boxing matches were fought outdoors on the ground. A circle was often drawn to mark the boundaries. **Spectators** would gather in a ring around the competitors.

Today, bouts occur indoors. Fighters stand on a raised platform that is about 3 to 4 feet (0.9 to 1.2 meters) above the floor. Although it is usually square in shape, the space in which the bout takes place is still known as a ring. Sometimes, it is called a "squared circle."

Traditionally, squared boxing rings had 24-foot (7.3-m) sides. The inside of a modern boxing ring typically measures 18 to 24 feet (5.4 to 7.3 m) on each side. The surface of the ring has 1 inch (2.5 cm) of padding. It is covered with a stretched canvas.

Each corner of the ring has a pole. Between the poles are four sets of ropes. The fighters are assigned to opposite corners. One fighter's corner is blue, and the other's is red. The remaining two corners are white. They are neutral corners. The **referee** stands in one of the neutral corners.

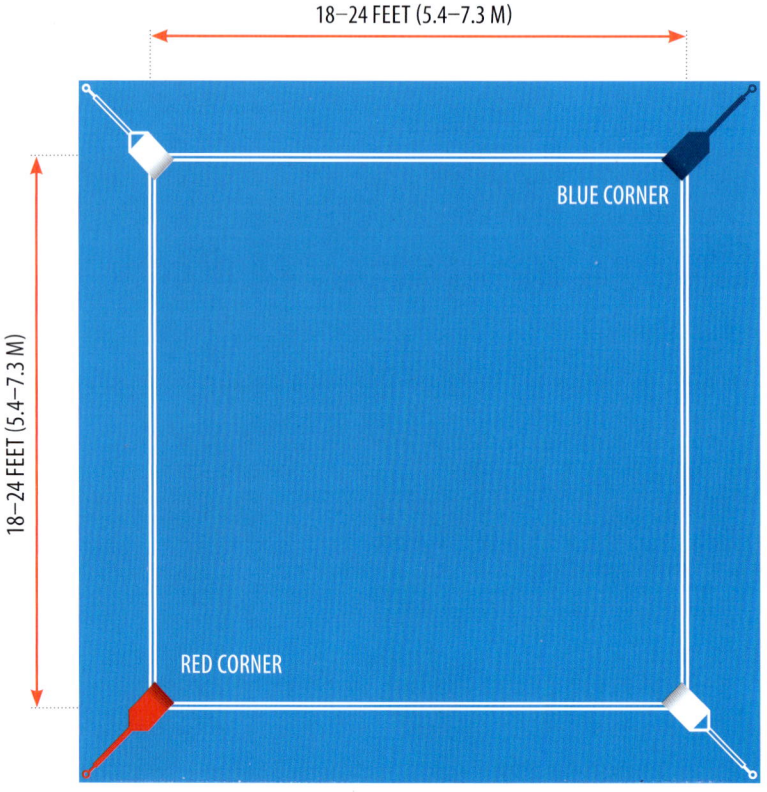

8 For the Love of Sports

Boxing Arenas

Some of the best-known boxing arenas are in major U.S. cities. The MGM Grand and Caesars Palace are two hotels in Las Vegas, Nevada, that are popular boxing venues. Madison Square Garden, in New York City, New York, is known as "The World's Most Famous Arena." This iconic venue has hosted some of the biggest live sporting and entertainment events of all time. Today, it often tops lists of the greatest boxing arenas in the world.

New York City, New York
One of the most memorable fights in Madison Square Garden took place on March 8, 1971. It is remembered as "The Fight of the Century" and was fought between Joe Frazier and Muhammad Ali. Other boxing legends to have fought at the Madison Square Garden Complex include "Sugar" Ray Robinson, Rocky Marciano, Jake LaMotta, Joe Louis, and Lennox Lewis.

Keeping Score

The main goal of boxing is to earn points by hitting an opponent while not taking any hits. Participants have multiple rounds in which to earn points. However, if a competitor is able to knock an opponent out, the fight is over, and he or she wins regardless of points.

There are two main types of scorekeeping. The method used depends on the level of the competitors. One kind of scoring is used in most amateur competitions. The other kind is used mainly for professional boxing matches.

For years, scoring at the Olympics followed the same method as amateur boxing. However, the 10-point system used in professional boxing has now been adopted. It was first used at the 2016 Olympics.

10   For the Love of Sports

In amateur boxing, scoring is based on the number of punches landed. Points are awarded for each hit. They must land on the midsection or the face. The person who lands the most successful strikes wins the round.

Professional boxing uses a 10-point system. The number of punches does not matter. Instead, scoring is based on rounds. After each round, the judges decide who fought the best. The winner of a round receives 10 points. The person who lost the round gets 9 points. Points can be deducted for illegal hits or being **knocked down**. At the end of a fight, the boxer with the most points wins.

Amateur boxing events usually have a panel of five judges. In order for a punch to count, it must be registered by at least three of them.

In a professional match, there are three ringside judges. They score each round and choose the winner.

Amateur boxing judges sometimes press buttons on a machine to register hits. These are then counted by a computer.

Boxing 11

Rules of the Ring

When boxing began, there were few rules. In ancient Greece, bouts were not split up into rounds. Instead, they went on until one of the participants yielded or became too injured to keep fighting. Most moves were permitted, even if they were likely to cause injury. It was common to continue attacking an opponent who had been thrown to the ground. Fighters could be hit anywhere on the body. All of this made boxing very dangerous.

In the mid-1700s, official rules forbidding certain actions were created. By the mid-1800s, even more rules were implemented. They made boxing much safer and brought fairness and structure to the sport. Fighters began wearing gloves, and a mandatory count was introduced for boxers unable to get up.

Today, there are many boxing rules. Striking an opponent below the belt is illegal, as are hits to the back, kidneys, neck, and back of the head.

Modern boxing rules regulate the types of moves that are allowed and dictate what gear must be worn in the ring.

12   For the Love of Sports

If someone breaks the rules, it is called a foul. The punishment for a foul can vary. Offenders may get a warning. They can also lose points. More serious fouls have harsher penalties, including a possible **disqualification**. A disqualified fighter automatically loses the round.

Boxers are not permitted to hold the ropes for support while punching.

Only punches made with closed fists are allowed in the ring. Fighters cannot hit with their heads, elbows, or forearms.

PUNCHES

KNOCKOUT

Fighters cannot hit an opponent who has been knocked down. Once a fighter is down, he or she has 10 seconds to get back up. If not, a knockout (KO) is declared.

Boxing 13

Amateurs and Professionals

Men's amateur and Olympic boxing matches typically have three rounds. Each round lasts for three minutes. In women's amateur and Olympic boxing, bouts last for four rounds. These rounds are two minutes long.

Most professional men's fights are 12 rounds long. In professional women's boxing, a match can go for up to 10 rounds. As in amateur boxing, rounds last three minutes each for men and two minutes each for women.

There is a one-minute rest period between every round of boxing. This is true for all matches, regardless of skill level or gender.

Norwegian boxer Cecilia Brækhus is known as the "First Lady of Boxing." She is the first woman to ever hold the four world title belts at the same time.

In the past, boxers of different sizes could fight each other. This put smaller fighters at a disadvantage. To make the sport more fair, weight divisions were introduced.

Originally, there was only one world champion for each weight class. Today, professional boxing is **sanctioned** by four organizations. These are the World Boxing Association (WBA), International Boxing Federation (IBF), World Boxing Council (WBC), and World Boxing Organization (WBO).

Each of the four sanctioning bodies awards title belts to world champions. This is why the current boxing period, which began in 2004, is known as the "four-belt era."

Fighters who hold two or more major title belts in a weight division are called unified champions. An undisputed champion is someone who holds all four major championship belts in a division.

Heavyweight is the highest weight class in men's professional boxing. Fighters must weigh more than 200 pounds (91 kilograms).

During the four-belt era, there has not been an undisputed heavyweight champion. British fighter Lennox Lewis was the last undisputed heavyweight champion. He earned the title in 1999.

Boxing 15

History of Boxing

Boxing has come a long way since its early beginnings. Today, this popular sport allows competitors to demonstrate their skill, speed, and strength.

Heavyweight boxing champion Jack Broughton was known as "the father of English boxing." He wrote the first formal set of boxing rules in 1743.

16 For the Love of Sports

688 BC — The first known official boxing event takes place. It is held in Greece during the 23rd Olympics.

1681 AD — The first boxing bout held in Great Britain is recorded. By the late 18th century, the sport is introduced to the United States.

1867 — The Marquess of Queensberry rules are first published in Great Britain. They were written by journalist and sportsman John Graham Chambers. These rules are still observed today.

1908 — Jack Johnson becomes the first African American world heavyweight champion.

2001 — At age 14, Giselle Salandy becomes the youngest person ever to win a world boxing title.

2021 — Claressa Shields becomes the first person in the four-belt era to win undisputed championships in two different weight divisions.

Cecilia Brækhus holds the Guinness World Record for **longest-reigning** female boxing world champion, at **11 years and 154 days**.

Manny Pacquiao is the only boxer to ever win world championships in **four different decades**.

In *2016*, *Christy Martin* became the **first woman** inducted into the *Nevada Boxing Hall of Fame*.

Boxing 17

Superstars of Boxing

There have been several amazing athletes in the world of boxing. They have inspired today's competitors.

Jack Dempsey
BIRTH DATE: June 24, 1895
HOMETOWN: Manassa, Colorado

CAREER FACTS:
- Dempsey started fighting under the name "Kid Blackie." He was taught to box by his older brother Bernie, a prizefighter who called himself Jack Dempsey. After filling in for Bernie in a match, he took over the name.
- On July 4, 1919, Dempsey became the world heavyweight champion. He beat Jess Willard and earned the nickname "The Manassa Mauler."
- He held the title of world heavyweight champion from 1919 to 1926.
- Dempsey's 1921 bout with French fighter Georges Carpentier was the first million-dollar **gate** in boxing.
- During his professional career, Dempsey fought in more than 80 bouts. He won 62 of them.
- Dempsey was inducted into the International Boxing Hall of Fame in 1990.

Joe Louis
BIRTH DATE: May 13, 1914
HOMETOWN: Lafayette, Alabama

CAREER FACTS:
- Louis was known by his nickname, "The Brown Bomber."
- As an amateur, Louis boxed in 54 bouts and won 50 of them. He turned pro in 1934 and did not lose a professional match until 1936.
- He held the world heavyweight champion title for more than 11 years in a row. This is still the longest for a champion in any weight division.
- Louis died in 1981 and was awarded a Congressional Gold Medal the following year.
- He was inducted into the International Boxing Hall of Fame in 1990.

"Sugar" Ray Robinson
BIRTH DATE: May 3, 1921
HOMETOWN: Detroit, Michigan

CAREER FACTS:
- Robinson's nickname came from his manager, George Gainford, who told a reporter that Robinson was as "sweet as sugar."
- As an amateur, Robinson was undefeated. He started boxing professionally in 1940.
- Robinson won his first 40 professional fights.
- He was a world welterweight champion at 147 pounds (67 kg). Robinson held this title from 1946 to 1951.
- At 160 pounds (73 kg), Robinson also became a world middleweight champion. He earned this title five times between 1951 and 1960.
- During his long career, Robinson fought in more than 200 professional bouts.

18   **For the Love of Sports**

Muhammad Ali
BIRTH DATE: January 17, 1942
HOMETOWN: Louisville, Kentucky

CAREER FACTS:
- Ali called himself "The Greatest." Many agreed and thought of him as the "People's Champion."
- As an amateur, he won a gold medal at the 1960 Olympics in the light heavyweight division. Years later, he lit the torch to open the 1996 Olympics.
- He was the first person ever to earn three world heavyweight champion titles.
- Ali had one of the best **jabs** in boxing. He was known for his footwork and speed.
- Ali was inducted into the International Boxing Hall of Fame in 1990.
- In 2005, Ali was awarded the Presidential Medal of Freedom.

Katie Taylor
BIRTH DATE: July 2, 1986
HOMETOWN: Bray, Ireland

CAREER FACTS:
- Taylor has had great success as both an amateur and professional boxer. She was named World Amateur Champion five times.
- She won an Olympic gold medal in 2012.
- In 2019, she became the undisputed world lightweight champion.
- Taylor is the first person to receive consecutive Boxing Writer Association of America (BWAA) Female Fighter of the Year awards. She won in both 2019 and 2020.
- She reached an undefeated 22–0 career record in 2022.

Lucia Rijker
BIRTH DATE: December 6, 1967
HOMETOWN: Amsterdam, Netherlands

CAREER FACTS:
- Rijker began martial arts training at age 6 and started kickboxing at age 15.
- She is undefeated in professional boxing, with a record of 17–0. Of these wins, 14 came by KO.
- Rijker's aggressive fighting style earned her nicknames such as "The Most Dangerous Woman in the World" and "The Dutch Destroyer."
- In 2020, she became one of the first three women inducted into the International Boxing Hall of Fame. The others were Christy Martin and Barbara Buttrick.

Saul "Canelo" Álvarez
BIRTH DATE: July 18, 1990
HOMETOWN: Guadalajara, Mexico

CAREER FACTS:
- Álvarez is widely considered the best active boxer in the world.
- His nickname "Canelo" comes from the Spanish word *canelito*. This means "little cinnamon." Álvarez's trainer gave him the nickname when he was 12 years old.
- Álvarez started boxing professionally in 2005 at age 15.
- He won 57 bouts between 2005 and 2021, with his only professional loss during that period coming in 2013 against legendary boxer Floyd Mayweather, Jr.
- Álvarez competes in several weight classes. In 2021, he became the first undisputed super middleweight champion.

Boxing 19

Staying Healthy

Boxers need a mixed diet. It should have **lean** proteins, healthy fats, and complex carbohydrates. Lean proteins include chicken, fish, and eggs. They help muscle tissue repair itself. Nuts and avocados have healthy fats. They help the body absorb nutrients. Complex carbohydrates provide raw energy. Some examples are pasta, quinoa, and whole wheat.

It is crucial for boxers to drink plenty of water. They should not wait until feeling thirsty to drink. Drinking water throughout the day will keep a boxer **hydrated**. It will also prevent aches and muscle cramps.

Boxers should always have a water bottle nearby. Experts recommend that boxers drink at least 1 gallon (3.8 liters) of water or more each day.

Some experts recommend that 35 to 60 percent of a boxer's daily diet should be made up of protein. Lean beef, shrimp, beans, and almonds are good choices.

It is important for boxers to train their hands. Successful fighters can punch efficiently, with grace and power. Speed bag drills build up endurance and coordination. Boxers must maintain a strong and consistent rhythm while punching. They should also focus on technique. Hitting a heavy bag can simulate a real fight. It provides a moving target.

Fighters need to train their feet as well. Interval training is a great workout for boxers. In interval training, high energy sprints are alternated with short periods of rest. Interval training mimics the way boxers must perform in the ring. Boxing is all about quick bursts of energy.

Training with a heavy bag helps boxers learn to dodge and block as they would when fighting a real opponent.

THE BOXING QUIZ

- **1** - Where did "The Fight of the Century" take place?

- **2** - When was **women's boxing** officially recognized as an **Olympic** sport?

- **3** - What is it called when someone **breaks a rule** in boxing?

- **4** - How long are the **rounds** in **men's boxing**?

- **5** - Where was the **first formal** boxing event held?

- **6** - Who was the **first** person to earn **three world heavyweight champion** titles?

- **7** - Which **two pieces** of **protective gear** are required for all boxers?

- **8** - Which three things should a **boxer's diet** include?

- **9** - How are **professional boxing** matches scored?

- **10** - Who was the **first African American** world heavyweight champion?

ANSWERS: 1 Madison Square Garden **2** 2012 **3** A foul **4** Three minutes each **5** Ancient Greece **6** Muhammad Ali **7** Gloves and mouthguards **8** Lean proteins, healthy fats, and complex carbohydrates **9** Using a 10-point system **10** Jack Johnson

22 **For the Love of Sports**

Key Words

amateur: a person who competes in a sport for fun or to win awards

bouts: boxing matches

competitors: people who face off against each other in events

disqualification: to become ineligible for a prize or competition due to breaking the rules

gate: the amount of money taken at a sporting venue through ticket sales

hydrated: provided with water to maintain a proper balance of fluids

jabs: straight punches from the forward-most hand

knocked down: when a boxer takes a punch and falls to the canvas, but can continue fighting

lean: a cut of meat with low fat

petroleum jelly: a mixture of mineral oils and waxes

prizefighting: a professional boxing contest with money as a prize

professional: a person who is paid to participate in a sport

referee: the person who makes sure the rules are followed during a match

sanctioned: officially approved by an authority

sparring: practicing boxing moves with an opponent

spectators: people who watch a sport but do not participate

Index

Ali, Muhammad 9, 19, 22
Álvarez, Saul "Canelo" 19
Brækhus, Cecilia 14, 17
Broughton, Jack 16
Dempsey, Jack 18
foul 13, 22
Frazier, Joe 9

International Boxing Federation (IBF) 15
Johnson, Jack 17, 22
knockout (KO) 4, 10, 13, 19
LaMotta, Jake 9
Lewis, Lennox 9, 15
Louis, Joe 9, 18
Marciano, Rocky 5, 9
Mayweather, Floyd, Jr. 19

Olympics 4, 5, 7, 10, 14, 17, 19, 22
points 4, 10, 11, 13, 22
punch 5, 6, 7, 11, 13, 21
Rijker, Lucia 19
ring 7, 8, 12, 13, 21
Robinson, "Sugar" Ray 9, 18

Salandy, Giselle 17
Shields, Claressa 5, 17
Taylor, Katie 19
World Boxing Association (WBA) 15
World Boxing Council (WBC) 15
World Boxing Organization (WBO) 15

Get the best of both worlds.

AV2 bridges the gap between print and digital.

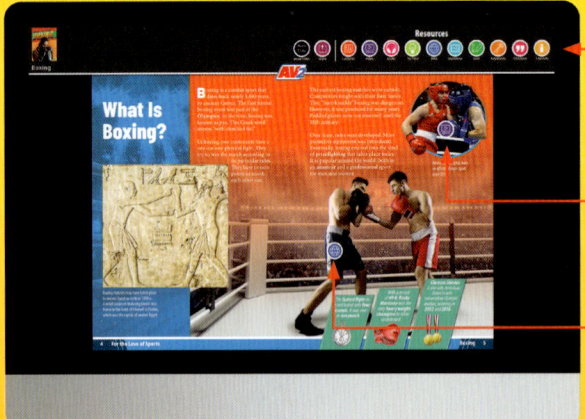

The expandable resources toolbar enables quick access to content including **videos**, **audio**, **activities**, **weblinks**, **slideshows**, **quizzes**, and **key words**.

Animated videos make static images come alive.

Resource icons on each page help readers to further **explore key concepts**.

Published by Lightbox Learning Inc.
276 5th Avenue, Suite 704 #917
New York, NY 10001
Website: www.openlightbox.com

Copyright ©2023 Lightbox Learning Inc.
All rights reserved. No part of this publication may be reproduced, stored in a retrieval system, or transmitted in any form or by any means, electronic, mechanical, photocopying, recording, or otherwise, without the prior written permission of the publisher.

Library of Congress Cataloging-in-Publication Data

Names: Gillespie, Katie, author.
Title: Boxing / Katie Gillespie.
Description: New York, NY : Lightbox Learning Inc., 2023. | Series: For the
   love of sports | Includes index. | Audience: Grades 4-6
Identifiers: LCCN 2022011689 (print) | LCCN 2022011690 (ebook) | ISBN
   9781791146016 (library binding) | ISBN 9781791146023 (paperback) | ISBN
   9781791146030
Subjects: LCSH: Boxing--Juvenile literatue.
Classification: LCC GV1136 .G55 2023 (print) | LCC GV1136 (ebook) | DDC
   796.83--dc23/eng/20220411
LC record available at https://lccn.loc.gov/2022011689
LC ebook record available at https://lccn.loc.gov/2022011690

Printed in Guangzhou, China
1 2 3 4 5 6 7 8 9 0 26 25 24 23 22

122022
101121

Project Coordinator Priyanka Das
Art Director Terry Paulhus
Layout Jean Faye Marie Rodriguez

Photo Credits
Every reasonable effort has been made to trace ownership and to obtain permission to reprint copyright material. The publisher would be pleased to have any errors or omissions brought to its attention so that they may be corrected in subsequent printings. The publisher acknowledges Alamy, Dreamstime, Getty Images, and Shutterstock as its primary image suppliers for this title.